Famous Explorers Bingo Book

COMPLETE BINGO GAME IN A BOOK

Written By Rebecca Stark

ISBN 978-0-87386-474-9

Educational Books 'n' Bingo

Printed in the U.S.A.

ADDITION BINGO DIRECTIONS

INCLUDED:

List of Terms

Templates for Additional Terms and Clues

2 Clues per Term

30 Unique Bingo Cards

Markers

1. **Either cut apart the book or make copies of ALL the sheets. You might want to make an extra copy of the clue sheets to use for introduction and review. Keep the sheets in an envelope for easy reuse.**

2. Cut apart the call cards with terms and clues.

3. Pass out one bingo card per student. There are enough for a class of 30.

4. Pass out markers. You may cut apart the markers included in this book or use any other small items of your choice.

5. Decide whether or not you will require the entire card to be filled. Requiring the entire card to be filled provides a better review. However, if you have a short time to fill, you may prefer to have them do the just the border or some other format. Tell the class before you begin what is required.

6. There are 50 terms. Read the list before you begin. If there are any terms that have not been covered in class, you may want to read to the students the term and clues before you begin.

7. There is a blank space in the middle of each card. You can instruct the students to use it as a free space or you can write in answers to cover terms not included. Of course, in this case you would create your own clues. (Templates provided.)

8. Shuffle the cards and place them in a pile. Two or three clues are provided for each term. If you plan to play the game with the same group more than once, you might want to choose a different clue for each game. If not, you may choose to use more than one clue.

9. Be sure to keep the cards you have used for the present game in a separate pile. When a student calls, "Bingo," he or she will have to verify that the correct answers are on his or her card AND that the markers were placed in response to the proper questions. Pull out the cards that are on the student's card keeping them in the order they were used in the game. Read each clue as it was given and ask the student to identify the correct answer from his or her card.

10. If the student has the correct answers on the card AND has shown that they were marked in response to the *correct questions,* then that student is the winner and the game is over. If the student does not have the correct answers on the card OR he or she marked the answers in response to *the wrong questions,* then the game continues until there is a proper winner.

11. If you want to play again, reshuffle the cards and begin again.

Have fun!

TERMS INCLUDED

Age of Discovery

Roald Amundsen

Neil Armstrong

astrolabe

Atahualpa

Aztec(s)

Vasco Núñez de Balboa

Vitus Bering

Richard E. Byrd

Álvar Núñez Cabeza de Vaca

John Cabot

Pedro Álvares Cabral

Juan Rodriguez Cabrillo

Antoine de la Mothe Cadillac

Cape of Good Hope

caravel

Jacques Cartier

cartography (cartographer)

Samuel de Champlain

Christopher Columbus

conquistador(s)

James Cook

Francisco Vásquez de Coronado

Corps of Discovery

Hernán Cortés

Vasco da Gama

Hernando de Soto

Bartolomeu Dias

Sir Francis Drake

Leif Ericsson

Yuri Alekseyevich Gagarin

Prince Henry the Navigator

Matthew Henson

Henry Hudson

Incan

Louis Joliet

Robert de la Salle

Bartolomé de las Casas

Ferdinand Magellan

Pedro Menéndez de Avilés

missions

Montezuma II

Northwest Passage

Francisco Pizarro

Marco Polo

Juan Ponce de León

Sir Walter Raleigh

Sacajawea

Giovanni da Verrazzano

Viking(s)

NOTE: Some names have alternative spellings.

Additional Terms

Choose as many additional terms as you would like and write them in the squares. Repeat each as desired.
Cut out the squares and randomly distribute them to the class.
Instruct the students to place their square on the center space of their card.

Explorers Bingo

Clues for Additional Terms

Write two clues for each of your additional terms.

1. _____ 2.	1. _____ 2.
1. _____ 2.	1. _____ 2. .
1. _____ 2.	1. _____ 2.

Age of Discovery 1. The period comprising the mid-to-late 15th and early 16th centuries in Europe is often referred to as the ___. 2. During the ___ many Europeans adventurers crossed the Atlantic Ocean to explore new lands.	**Roald Amundsen** 1. In December 1911 this Norwegian polar explorer became the first person to reach the South Pole. 2. This Norwegian explorer was the first to navigate a ship through the Northwest Passage.
Neil Armstrong 1. He became the first person to step on the moon on July 20, 1969. 2. As he stepped off the lunar module, he said, "That's one small step for man, one giant leap for mankind." Interesting Fact: He meant to say "one small step for a man."	**astrolabe** 1. This device was used by explorers to determine their location. 2. The ___ helped explorers determine where they were using the positions of the stars or sun.
Atahualpa 1. ___ was the last ruler of the Inca Empire. 2. He was captured by conquistadors led any Francisco Pizarro and was killed in 1533.	**Aztec(s)** 1. Spanish conquistador Hernán Cortés and his men overthrew the ___ Empire in 1521. 2. Their magnificent capital city, Tenochtitlán, was the site of the future Mexico City.
Vasco Núñez de Balboa 1. This Spanish explorer, governor, and conquistador crossed the Isthmus of Panama to the Pacific Ocean in 1513. 2. He was the first European to see the Pacific Ocean.	**Vitus Bering** 1. Although born in Denmark, ___ joined the Russian navy. In 1741 he became the first European to discover Alaska and its Aleutian Islands. 2. The waterway between Asia and North America is named for him.
Richard E. Byrd 1. This aviator, naval officer, and pilot is best known for his explorations of Antarctica and the polar regions. 2. During his 1928 expedition to Antarctica, a base camp named "Little America" was constructed on the Ross Ice Shelf.	**Álvar Núñez Cabeza de Vaca** 1. He was one of only 4 survivors of the 1527 expedition led by Panfilo de Narvaez. Another survivor was Estevanico, also known as Esteban the Moor. 2. In 1537 he wrote about his 8-year expedition across Texas. This report aroused Spanish interest in Texas.

John Cabot
1. This Italian-born English explorer was the first European since the Vikings to explore the mainland of North America and the first to search for the Northwest Passage. He made his first voyage in 1497.
2. His son Sebastian was also an explorer.

Pedro Álvares Cabral
1. This Portuguese navigator is considered the discoverer of Brazil.
2. In 1500 King Manuel I sent ___ on an expedition to India. On April 22 ___ claimed the land he sighted for Portugal and named it Island of the True Cross. The king changed it to Holy Cross. It was later named Brazil.

Juan Rodriguez Cabrillo
1. In 1542 he led the first European expedition to explore the present-day west coast of the United States for Spain.
2. ___ is known as the discoverer of California.

Antoine de la Mothe Cadillac
1. In 1701 this French explorer established a Great Lakes fur-trading post and founded Fort Pontchartrain du Détroit (Fort Detroit).
2. An automobile was named after this founder of Detroit.

Cape of Good Hope
1. This rocky promontory on the Atlantic coast of the Cape Peninsula, South Africa, was first sighted by Bartolomeu Dias in 1488 on his return voyage to Portugal.
2. It was so named because it was a sign that India could be reached by sea from Europe. Some say Dias first named it Cape of Storms.

caravel
1. This sailing ship, developed by the Portuguese in the late 1400s, was relatively small and light.
2. The ___ had 2 or 3 masts with square sails as well as a triangular sail.

Jacques Cartier
1. This French explorer explored the St. Lawrence River. In 1534 he was sent by King Francis I to the New World in search of riches and a new route to Asia.
2. His explorations of the Canadian coast and the St. Lawrence River laid the basis for later French claims to North America.

cartography (cartographer)
1. ___ is the art and science of making maps. Important advances in this science were made during the Age of Exploration.
2. Christopher Columbus worked with his brother in Lisbon as a ___, or mapmaker.

Samuel de Champlain
1. This French explorer and navigator mapped a large portion of northeastern North America.
2. He founded New France and Quebec City in 1608 and is sometimes called Father of New France or Father of Canada.

Christopher Columbus
1. Born in Genoa, Italy, he made 4 voyages across the Atlantic Ocean for the Spanish monarchs Queen Isabella and King Ferdinand. The first was made in 1492.
2. During his first voyage he led 3 Spanish galleons, the *Niña,* the *Pinta,* and the *Santa Maria.*

© **Barbara M Peller**

conquistador(s)	**James Cook**
1. This term means "conqueror" and refers to a leader in the Spanish conquest of America, especially of Mexico and Peru. 2. The ___ of the 16th century were after wealth and power. In general, they exploited the natives they encountered.	1. A captain in the Royal Navy, this 18th-century British explorer made the first recorded European contact with the eastern coastline of Australia and the Hawaiian Islands. 2. ___ was killed in Hawaii during his third exploratory voyage in the Pacific in 1779.
Francisco Vásquez de Coronado	**Corps of Discovery**
1. He unsuccessfully searched for the treasure that was said to exist in northern Mexico: the mythical Seven Golden Cities of Cibola. 2. This Spanish conquistador visited parts of what are now the southwestern United States between 1540 and 1542.	1. ___ was the name given to the Lewis and Clark Expedition. It was led by Meriwether Lewis and William Clark. 2. One purpose of this expedition was to gain knowledge of the lands acquired by the Louisiana Purchase. The expedition began May 14, 1804.
Hernán Cortés	**Vasco da Gama**
1. This Spanish conquistador led the expedition that resulted in the fall of the Aztec Empire. 2. By overthrowing the Aztec empire in 1521, he won Mexico for Spain.	1. This Portuguese explorer ___ was the first to go directly from Europe to India. 2. This Portuguese explorer became Governor of India in 1524.
Hernando de Soto	**Bartolomeu Dias**
1. In 1541 this Spanish explorer and his men became the first Europeans to cross the Mississippi River. 2. Although not the first European to discover Florida, he and his men were the first to explore it and other parts of southeastern U.S. In 1531 he went with Pizarro on his expedition to Peru.	1. In 1487, King John II of Portugal ordered him to sail to the southern end of Africa. The king wanted to know if ships could reach Asia by sailing around Africa. 2. He was the first European to sail around the Cape of Good Hope.
Sir Francis Drake	**Leif Ericsson**
1. This English admiral circumnavigated the globe in 1577–1578, but he was not the first to do so. 2. This English admiral helped defeat the Spanish Armada in 1588.	1. This Norse explorer is believed to have been the first European to land in North America. He is said to have come to the shores of northeastern America in the year 1000. 2. His father, Eric the Red, is said to have founded the first Norse settlement in Greenland.

Explorers Bingo

Yuri Alekseyevich Gagarin 1. ___ was a Russian-Soviet pilot and cosmonaut. 2. He became the first human to journey into outer space on April 12, 1961.	**Prince Henry the Navigator** 1. This son of King John I of Portugal is best known as a patron of explorers. 2. Although this son of King John I never sailed on any expeditions and rarely left Portugal, he became known as ___. He lived from 1394–1460.
Matthew Henson 1. ___ was part of the expedition led by Robert Peary; he, Peary, and four Eskimos became the first people to reach the North Pole on April 6, 1909. 2. He was the first African-American to explore the Arctic.	**Henry Hudson** 1. This English sea explorer hoped to discover an ice-free waterway from Europe to Asia. One of his ships was the *Half Moon*. 2. During his third voyage to the New World in 1609, he discovered the river that would be named for him. On his fourth voyage, he sailed through the strait and the bay also named for him.
Incan 1. Machu Picchu was abandoned when the ___ Empire was conquered by the Spaniards in the 16th century. 2. The ___ Empire ended in 1532 when Francisco Pizarro had Atahualpa, the last ___ emperor, killed.	**Louis Joliet** 1. This 17th-century Canadian explorer explored the origins of the Mississippi River. 2. In 1673 he accompanied missionary Jacques Marquette on an expedition.
Robert de la Salle 1. On April 9, 1682, ___ proclaimed the whole Mississippi Basin for France. 2. ___ named the region he explored and claimed Louisiana after King Louis XIV of France.	**Bartolomé de las Casas** 1. This Spanish Dominican missionary became known for his defense of the rights of the native people of the Americas. 2. In 1542 he wrote "A Short Account of the Destruction of the Indies," which described the mistreatment of the indigenous peoples of the Americas.
Ferdinand Magellan 1. This Portuguese explorer was sailing for Spain when he organized the expedition that resulted in the first circumnavigation of the Earth. 2. Although some of his crew completed the first circumnavigation of the Earth, ___ died before the voyage was completed.	**Pedro Menéndez de Avilés** 1. This Spanish conquistador founded St. Augustine, Florida, in 1565. It is the oldest continually inhabited city in the US. 2. King Philip II sent ___ to Florida to take the land from the French who had settled there. ___ captured the French colony of Fort Caroline and murdered the entire population.

Explorers Bingo

missions 1. One purpose of the Spanish ___ that were established along the California coast was to convert the native people to the Catholic faith. 2. Father Serra had established 9 ___ when he died in 1784. By 1823 a total of 21 ___ were built.	**Montezuma II** 1. Montezuma II was the last ruler of the Aztec Empire. 2. He was defeated by the Spanish conquistador Hernán Cortés in 1520.
Northwest Passage 1. For centuries explorers tried to find a route from the Atlantic Ocean to the Pacific Ocean through the Arctic archipelago of present-day Canada. This route is known as the ___. 2. Roald Amundsen was the first to make a ship voyage through the ___.	**Francisco Pizarro** 1. This Spanish conquistador conquered Peru and founded Lima, its capital city. 2. ___ ruled Peru for 10 years before he was assassinated in Lima in 1541 by rival conquistadors.
Marco Polo 1. In 1271, the Venetian merchant ___ embarked on a 24-year journey across Asia. 2. Although written in the 13th century, *The Travels of* ___ had a great influence on Columbus and other later explorers.	**Juan Ponce de León** 1. In 1513 this Spanish explorer became the first European to discover Florida. He is known for his search for the Fountain of Youth. 2. In 1508 and 1508 he explored Puerto Rico and founded Caparra, its oldest settlement. He was Puerto Rico's first governor.
Sir Walter Raleigh 1. This English explorer established a colony near Roanoke Island. 2. Although it is often said that this English explorer introduced potatoes and tobacco to Britain, these products were already known because of the Spanish explorers.	**Sacajawea** 1. This Shoshone woman accompanied the Lewis and Clark Expedition and became a valuable member. 2. She acted as an interpreter and guide on the Lewis and Clark Expedition to explore western lands.
Giovanni da Verrazzano 1. This Italian explorer sailed for France. He explored the eastern coast of North America. His discoveries include the sites of present-day New York Harbor, Block Island, & Narragansett Bay. 2. The bridge that connects the New York City boroughs of Staten Island and Brooklyn is named for this Italian explorer.	**Viking(s)** 1. This name refers to the Scandinavian seafaring warriors of the late 8th through the 11th centuries. 2. Eric the Red was a ___ explorer; he was the first European to sail to Greenland.

Explorers Bingo

Explorers Bingo

Bartolomé de las Casas	Age of Discovery	Neil Armstrong	conquistador(s)	Atahualpa
Samuel de Champlain	Roald Amundsen	Sacajawea	Yuri Alekseyevich Gagarin	Marco Polo
Sir Walter Raleigh	Leif Ericsson		Incan	Giovanni da Verrazzano
Juan Ponce de León	missions	Francisco Pizarro	Sir Francis Drake	Matthew Henson
Henry Hudson	Corps of Discovery	caravel	Montezuma II	Richard E. Byrd

Explorers Bingo: Card No. 1

Explorers Bingo

Juan Ponce de León	Sir Walter Raleigh	Vasco da Gama	Ferdinand Magellan	Bartolomeu Dias
Matthew Henson	Jacques Cartier	Vitus Bering	missions	Pedro Álvares Cabral
John Cabot	Corps of Discovery		Hernán Cortés	Francisco Pizarro
Louis Joliet	Robert de la Salle	Leif Ericsson	Viking(s)	Atahualpa
Marco Polo	Sacajawea	caravel	Samuel de Champlain	Montezuma II

Explorers Bingo

Corps of Discovery	Francisco Pizarro	Jacques Cartier	Sir Francis Drake	Sir Walter Raleigh
Matthew Henson	Roald Amundsen	Álvar Núñez Cabeza de Vaca	Age of Discovery	Francisco Vásquez de Coronado
missions	Sacajawea		Pedro Álvares Cabral	astrolabe
Leif Ericsson	John Cabot	Henry Hudson	Louis Joliet	Vasco da Gama
Montezuma II	Juan Rodriguez Cabrillo	caravel	Viking(s)	Bartolomeu Dias

Explorers Bingo

Leif Ericsson	Pedro Álvares Cabral	Neil Armstrong	Juan Rodriguez Cabrillo	Bartolomeu Dias
Prince Henry the Navigator	Vasco Núñez de Balboa	Age of Discovery	Ferdinand Magellan	Sir Walter Raleigh
Incan	Louis Joliet		Richard E. Byrd	conquistador(s)
Francisco Pizarro	Roald Amundsen	Sacajawea	caravel	Vitus Bering
Antoine de la Mothe Cadillac	Marco Polo	Aztec(s)	Montezuma II	Giovanni da Verrazzano

Explorers Bingo: Card No. 4

Explorers Bingo

Marco Polo	Atahualpa	missions	Vitus Bering	Juan Rodriguez Cabrillo
Prince Henry the Navigator	Francisco Pizarro	Álvar Núñez Cabeza de Vaca	Hernán Cortés	Roald Amundsen
Neil Armstrong	Giovanni da Verrazzano		Yuri Alekseyevich Gagarin	James Cook
Richard E. Byrd	Bartolomeu Dias	Bartolomé de las Casas	Viking(s)	Cape of Good Hope
Jacques Cartier	caravel	Sir Walter Raleigh	Leif Ericsson	Incan

Explorers Bingo: Card No. 5

Explorers Bingo

astrolabe	Pedro Álvares Cabral	Vasco da Gama	Bartolomeu Dias	Giovanni da Verrazzano
Sir Francis Drake	missions	Cape of Good Hope	Age of Discovery	Sir Walter Raleigh
Ferdinand Magellan	Antoine de la Mothe Cadillac		Vasco Núñez de Balboa	Hernán Cortés
caravel	Henry Hudson	Viking(s)	Aztec(s)	Neil Armstrong
Matthew Henson	Vitus Bering	Bartolomé de las Casas	Incan	cartography (cartographer)

Explorers Bingo

Bartolomé de las Casas	Pedro Álvares Cabral	James Cook	Francisco Pizarro	Jacques Cartier
Matthew Henson	Bartolomeu Dias	Corps of Discovery	Roald Amundsen	Prince Henry the Navigator
Giovanni da Verrazzano	conquistador(s)		Hernán Cortés	Vasco Núñez de Balboa
Leif Ericsson	Louis Joliet	Álvar Núñez Cabeza de Vaca	Juan Ponce de León	John Cabot
caravel	Juan Rodriguez Cabrillo	Viking(s)	Aztec(s)	astrolabe

Explorers Bingo

Incan	Pedro Álvares Cabral	Christopher Columbus	Sir Francis Drake	Vasco Núñez de Balboa
Prince Henry the Navigator	Neil Armstrong	Ferdinand Magellan	Giovanni da Verrazzano	Vitus Bering
cartography (cartographer)	Juan Rodriguez Cabrillo		Bartolomeu Dias	Atahualpa
Montezuma II	Leif Ericsson	Juan Ponce de León	Antoine de la Mothe Cadillac	Louis Joliet
Sacajawea	caravel	Aztec(s)	missions	Matthew Henson

Explorers Bingo: Card No. 8

Explorers Bingo

Hernán Cortés	Jacques Cartier	Corps of Discovery	cartography (cartographer)	Juan Rodriguez Cabrillo
Antoine de la Mothe Cadillac	Bartolomeu Dias	Incan	missions	Pedro Álvares Cabral
Francisco Vásquez de Coronado	Bartolomé de las Casas		Roald Amundsen	Christopher Columbus
Cape of Good Hope	Atahualpa	Henry Hudson	Yuri Alekseyevich Gagarin	James Cook
Louis Joliet	Viking(s)	Álvar Núñez Cabeza de Vaca	Juan Ponce de León	Richard E. Byrd

Explorers Bingo: Card No. 9

Explorers Bingo

Juan Ponce de León	Sir Francis Drake	Vasco Núñez de Balboa	Ferdinand Magellan	cartography (cartographer)
Giovanni da Verrazzano	Vitus Bering	Age of Discovery	Roald Amundsen	Bartolomeu Dias
Juan Rodriguez Cabrillo	Pedro Álvares Cabral		conquistador(s)	John Cabot
Henry Hudson	Richard E. Byrd	Cape of Good Hope	Viking(s)	Francisco Vásquez de Coronado
Álvar Núñez Cabeza de Vaca	Matthew Henson	Vasco da Gama	Marco Polo	Incan

Explorers Bingo

astrolabe	Pedro Álvares Cabral	missions	Cape of Good Hope	Matthew Henson
Christopher Columbus	Francisco Vásquez de Coronado	Yuri Alekseyevich Gagarin	Hernán Cortés	Age of Discovery
Prince Henry the Navigator	Bartolomeu Dias		Vasco da Gama	Corps of Discovery
Álvar Núñez Cabeza de Vaca	Sir Walter Raleigh	Viking(s)	Juan Rodriguez Cabrillo	Juan Ponce de León
Antoine de la Mothe Cadillac	caravel	Bartolomé de las Casas	Aztec(s)	Jacques Cartier

Explorers Bingo

Jacques Cartier	Atahualpa	Francisco Vásquez de Coronado	Sir Francis Drake	Hernán Cortés
Corps of Discovery	Matthew Henson	Neil Armstrong	Aztec(s)	Roald Amundsen
Bartolomé de las Casas	James Cook		Giovanni da Verrazzano	Ferdinand Magellan
caravel	Louis Joliet	Bartolomeu Dias	Juan Ponce de León	Prince Henry the Navigator
Pedro Álvares Cabral	Christopher Columbus	Juan Rodriguez Cabrillo	Antoine de la Mothe Cadillac	Vitus Bering

Explorers Bingo

Cape of Good Hope	Atahualpa	astrolabe	Francisco Vásquez de Coronado	Giovanni da Verrazzano
Neil Armstrong	Christopher Columbus	Bartolomeu Dias	Hernán Cortés	John Cabot
Sir Francis Drake	Vitus Bering		Corps of Discovery	James Cook
Incan	Viking(s)	Vasco Núñez de Balboa	Juan Rodriguez Cabrillo	Juan Ponce de León
caravel	Richard E. Byrd	Aztec(s)	Bartolomé de las Casas	Yuri Alekseyevich Gagarin

Explorers Bingo

Samuel de Champlain	Bartolomeu Dias	missions	Hernán Cortés	Antoine de la Mothe Cadillac
Vitus Bering	Bartolomé de las Casas	Francisco Vásquez de Coronado	Roald Amundsen	Pedro Álvares Cabral
Cape of Good Hope	conquistador(s)		Vasco da Gama	Álvar Núñez Cabeza de Vaca
Richard E. Byrd	Viking(s)	Juan Rodriguez Cabrillo	Vasco Núñez de Balboa	astrolabe
caravel	Ferdinand Magellan	John Cabot	Matthew Henson	Incan

Explorers Bingo: Card No. 14

Explorers Bingo

Yuri Alekseyevich Gagarin	Hernán Cortés	missions	Jacques Cartier	Sir Francis Drake
astrolabe	Vasco da Gama	Age of Discovery	Neil Armstrong	Antoine de la Mothe Cadillac
Giovanni da Verrazzano	Bartolomé de las Casas		Sir Walter Raleigh	Pedro Álvares Cabral
caravel	Francisco Vásquez de Coronado	Christopher Columbus	Viking(s)	Cape of Good Hope
Matthew Henson	Louis Joliet	Aztec(s)	cartography (cartographer)	Corps of Discovery

Explorers Bingo

Vasco Núñez de Balboa	Francisco Vásquez de Coronado	Christopher Columbus	cartography (cartographer)	Robert de la Salle
Ferdinand Magellan	John Cabot	James Cook	Prince Henry the Navigator	conquistador(s)
Cape of Good Hope	Atahualpa		Giovanni da Verrazzano	Corps of Discovery
Leif Ericsson	Vitus Bering	caravel	Yuri Alekseyevich Gagarin	Juan Ponce de León
Antoine de la Mothe Cadillac	Northwest Passage	Aztec(s)	Louis Joliet	Pedro Álvares Cabral

Explorers Bingo

Álvar Núñez Cabeza de Vaca	Pedro Menéndez de Avilés	Hernando de Soto	Francisco Vásquez de Coronado	Samuel de Champlain
Yuri Alekseyevich Gagarin	Antoine de la Mothe Cadillac	Viking(s)	conquistador(s)	James Cook
Hernán Cortés	Incan		Northwest Passage	Christopher Columbus
Richard E. Byrd	Matthew Henson	Juan Ponce de León	missions	John Cabot
Henry Hudson	Cape of Good Hope	Jacques Cartier	Sir Francis Drake	Atahualpa

Explorers Bingo

cartography (cartographer)	Juan Rodriguez Cabrillo	Vitus Bering	Cape of Good Hope	Ferdinand Magellan
Pedro Álvares Cabral	Álvar Núñez Cabeza de Vaca	Henry Hudson	Giovanni da Verrazzano	Antoine de la Mothe Cadillac
Hernán Cortés	John Cabot		Hernando de Soto	Neil Armstrong
Atahualpa	Age of Discovery	Viking(s)	Juan Ponce de León	Vasco da Gama
Northwest Passage	Francisco Vásquez de Coronado	missions	Pedro Menéndez de Avilés	astrolabe

Explorers Bingo

Giovanni da Verrazzano	astrolabe	Francisco Vásquez de Coronado	Christopher Columbus	Juan Ponce de León
Yuri Alekseyevich Gagarin	Sir Francis Drake	Pedro Álvares Cabral	Jacques Cartier	conquistador(s)
Pedro Menéndez de Avilés	Juan Rodriguez Cabrillo		Roald Amundsen	Sir Walter Raleigh
Vasco da Gama	Northwest Passage	Henry Hudson	Louis Joliet	Hernando de Soto
Neil Armstrong	Robert de la Salle	Matthew Henson	Incan	Aztec(s)

Explorers Bingo

Samuel de Champlain	Pedro Menéndez de Avilés	Sir Francis Drake	Francisco Vásquez de Coronado	Aztec(s)
Vitus Bering	Corps of Discovery	Prince Henry the Navigator	Henry Hudson	Ferdinand Magellan
Atahualpa	James Cook		Leif Ericsson	Age of Discovery
Marco Polo	Sacajawea	Montezuma II	Louis Joliet	Northwest Passage
Francisco Pizarro	Incan	Robert de la Salle	Juan Ponce de León	Hernando de Soto

Explorers Bingo

Yuri Alekseyevich Gagarin	astrolabe	Prince Henry the Navigator	Francisco Vásquez de Coronado	Marco Polo
Atahualpa	Hernando de Soto	Vasco Núñez de Balboa	Christopher Columbus	Bartolomé de las Casas
John Cabot	Matthew Henson		Pedro Menéndez de Avilés	missions
Henry Hudson	Jacques Cartier	Northwest Passage	Richard E. Byrd	Incan
Leif Ericsson	Robert de la Salle	Aztec(s)	Álvar Núñez Cabeza de Vaca	Louis Joliet

Explorers Bingo

cartography (cartographer)	Vasco da Gama	Hernando de Soto	Neil Armstrong	Cape of Good Hope
Ferdinand Magellan	Sir Francis Drake	Sir Walter Raleigh	Christopher Columbus	Roald Amundsen
Vitus Bering	conquistador(s)		Bartolomé de las Casas	James Cook
Northwest Passage	Richard E. Byrd	Louis Joliet	Age of Discovery	Prince Henry the Navigator
Robert de la Salle	Álvar Núñez Cabeza de Vaca	Pedro Menéndez de Avilés	John Cabot	Leif Ericsson

Explorers Bingo

Vasco Núñez de Balboa	Pedro Menéndez de Avilés	Jacques Cartier	Neil Armstrong	Aztec(s)
astrolabe	Samuel de Champlain	Matthew Henson	Yuri Alekseyevich Gagarin	Age of Discovery
Vasco da Gama	Cape of Good Hope		Montezuma II	Bartolomé de las Casas
John Cabot	Robert de la Salle	Northwest Passage	Álvar Núñez Cabeza de Vaca	Louis Joliet
Marco Polo	Sacajawea	Incan	Henry Hudson	Hernando de Soto

Explorers Bingo: Card No. 23

Explorers Bingo

Vasco Núñez de Balboa	Incan	Samuel de Champlain	Pedro Menéndez de Avilés	Christopher Columbus
Hernando de Soto	Aztec(s)	Prince Henry the Navigator	Ferdinand Magellan	Bartolomé de las Casas
James Cook	cartography (cartographer)		Cape of Good Hope	John Cabot
Marco Polo	Montezuma II	Northwest Passage	Álvar Núñez Cabeza de Vaca	Atahualpa
Francisco Pizarro	Leif Ericsson	Robert de la Salle	Sir Francis Drake	Sacajawea

Explorers Bingo

Leif Ericsson	Prince Henry the Navigator	Pedro Menéndez de Avilés	missions	Hernando de Soto
Age of Discovery	Atahualpa	Yuri Alekseyevich Gagarin	Vasco Núñez de Balboa	Roald Amundsen
Richard E. Byrd	Christopher Columbus		Montezuma II	Northwest Passage
Sir Walter Raleigh	Marco Polo	Sacajawea	Robert de la Salle	conquistador(s)
Aztec(s)	Samuel de Champlain	Vitus Bering	Antoine de la Mothe Cadillac	Francisco Pizarro

Explorers Bingo

Hernando de Soto	Pedro Menéndez de Avilés	Vasco da Gama	Ferdinand Magellan	cartography (cartographer)
Henry Hudson	Sir Francis Drake	Christopher Columbus	Samuel de Champlain	Vasco Núñez de Balboa
Richard E. Byrd	Montezuma II		conquistador(s)	Leif Ericsson
Álvar Núñez Cabeza de Vaca	Neil Armstrong	Marco Polo	Robert de la Salle	Northwest Passage
James Cook	Antoine de la Mothe Cadillac	missions	Sacajawea	Francisco Pizarro

Explorers Bingo

Vasco da Gama	Vitus Bering	Pedro Menéndez de Avilés	Samuel de Champlain	Corps of Discovery
Marco Polo	Montezuma II	Yuri Alekseyevich Gagarin	Northwest Passage	Roald Amundsen
Viking(s)	Sacajawea		Robert de la Salle	Leif Ericsson
cartography (cartographer)	astrolabe	Prince Henry the Navigator	Francisco Pizarro	Age of Discovery
Antoine de la Mothe Cadillac	conquistador(s)	Hernando de Soto	Sir Walter Raleigh	James Cook

Explorers Bingo

Vasco da Gama	Samuel de Champlain	Sir Walter Raleigh	Pedro Menéndez de Avilés	Vasco Núñez de Balboa
Corps of Discovery	Hernando de Soto	Montezuma II	Ferdinand Magellan	conquistador(s)
Sacajawea	John Cabot		James Cook	Henry Hudson
Juan Ponce de León	cartography (cartographer)	Matthew Henson	Robert de la Salle	Northwest Passage
Neil Armstrong	Hernán Cortés	Antoine de la Mothe Cadillac	Francisco Pizarro	Marco Polo

Explorers Bingo: Card No. 28

Explorers Bingo

Hernando de Soto	Samuel de Champlain	cartography (cartographer)	Yuri Alekseyevich Gagarin	Hernán Cortés
Louis Joliet	Henry Hudson	Prince Henry the Navigator	James Cook	Sir Walter Raleigh
Richard E. Byrd	Montezuma II		Roald Amundsen	Pedro Menéndez de Avilés
Corps of Discovery	Marco Polo	Bartolomeu Dias	Robert de la Salle	Northwest Passage
Vasco Núñez de Balboa	Christopher Columbus	Francisco Pizarro	astrolabe	Sacajawea

Explorers Bingo: Card No. 29

Explorers Bingo

Juan Rodriguez Cabrillo	Pedro Menéndez de Avilés	Ferdinand Magellan	Hernán Cortés	Northwest Passage
Age of Discovery	Samuel de Champlain	Vasco da Gama	conquistador(s)	Roald Amundsen
Richard E. Byrd	Cape of Good Hope		James Cook	Prince Henry the Navigator
Francisco Pizarro	astrolabe	Neil Armstrong	Robert de la Salle	Montezuma II
Marco Polo	Giovanni da Verrazzano	Sacajawea	Hernando de Soto	Sir Walter Raleigh